To

From

Aunt Cate

Date

5/26/08

Jojo

AuntCate

5/26/08

Purpose
for
Everyday Living

for

Teens

Simon & Schuster, Inc.
1230 Avenue of the Americas, New York, NY 10020

*The quoted ideas expressed in this book (but not Scripture verses) are not, in all cases,
exact quotations, as some have been edited for clarity and brevity. In all cases, the author
has attempted to maintain the speaker's original intent. In some cases, quoted material
for this book was obtained from secondary sources, primarily print media. While every
effort was made to ensure the accuracy of these sources, the accuracy cannot be guaran-
teed. For additions, deletions, corrections, or clarifications in future editions of this text,
please write Freeman-Smith, LLC.*

Scripture quotations marked NCV are taken from the New Century Version®.
Copyright © 1987, 1988, 1991 by Thomas Nelson, Inc. Used by permission.
All rights reserved.

Scripture quotations marked NKJV are taken from The Holy Bible, New
King James Version. Copyright © 1982, 1988 by Thomas Nelson, Inc. All
rights reserved.

Scriptures marked KJV are taken from the *Holy Bible, King James Version.*

Cover Design & Page Layout by Bart Dawson

Manufactured in the United States of America

10 9 8 7 6 5 4 3

ISBN-13: 978-1-4169-4840-7
ISBN-10: 1-4169-4840-6

Purpose
for
Everyday Living

for Teens

Simon & Schuster, Inc.
NEW YORK LONDON TORONTO SYDNEY

Table of Contents

Introduction

God gave you a life, and now you've got to decide what to do with it. But sometimes, deciding what to do is difficult. This book is intended to help.

God has a plan for everything, including you. As a part of that plan, He intends that you experience abundance and joy in this life *and* throughout all eternity. But perhaps *your* vision of God's plan is not quite as clear as you would like. If so, the ideas on these pages will help you discover God's purpose for your life.

This text does not attempt to answer every question concerning your particular situation; instead, it gives you Biblically-based, time-tested principles that can serve as directions for the journey ahead.

If you genuinely seek God's guidance, He will give it. But, He will make His revelations known to you in a way and in a time of *His* choosing, not yours. So, if you're seeking to know God's will for your life, don't be worried if you haven't yet received a "final" answer. The final answer, of course, will come not in this world, but in the next. In the meantime, keep watching for God's signs and studying God's Word. When you sincerely seek His will—and keep seeking it—He will direct your path to a place of joyful abundance and eternal peace.

Chapter 1

Why Am I Here?

You will show me the path of life . . . .
Psalm 16:11 NKJV

"What on earth does God intend for me to do with my life?" It's an easy question to ask but, for many of us, a difficult question to answer. Why? Because God's purposes aren't always clear to us. Sometimes we wander aimlessly in a wilderness of our own making. And sometimes, we struggle mightily against God in a vain effort to find success and happiness through our own means, not His.

Whenever we struggle against God's will and His plans for our lives, we suffer. When we resist God's calling, our efforts bear little fruit. But, when we align ourselves with God's purposes, we soon discover that He is a source of courage and strength. When we align ourselves with God's purposes, we avail ourselves of His power and His peace.

How can we know precisely what God's intentions are? The answer, of course, is that even the most well-intentioned believers face periods of uncertainty and doubt about the direction of their lives. So, too, will you.

When you arrive at one of life's inevitable crossroads, that is precisely the moment when you should turn your thoughts and prayers toward God. When you do, He will make Himself known to you in a time and manner of His choosing.

Are you earnestly seeking to discern God's purpose for your life? If so, this book is intended to remind you of several important facts:

1. God has a plan for your life;

2. If you seek that plan sincerely and prayerfully, you will find it;

3. When you discover God's purpose for your life, you will experience abundance, peace, joy, and power—God's power. And that's the only kind of power that really matters.

Continually restate to yourself what
the purpose of your life is.

Oswald Chambers

The born-again Christian sees life not
as a blurred, confused, meaningless mass,
but as something planned and purposeful.

Billy Graham

You are God's chief creation,
and you are here for His pleasure
and His glory.

Beth Moore

We are all pencils in the hand of God.

Mother Teresa

More people fail from lack of purpose
than lack of talent.

Billy Sunday

The study of inspired Scripture
is the chief way of finding our duty.

St. Basil the Great

We must focus on prayer as the main thrust
to accomplish God's will and purpose on
earth. The forces against us have never been
greater, and this is the only way we can
release God's power to become victorious.

John Maxwell

If the Lord calls you, He will equip you
for the task He wants you to fulfill.

Warren Wiersbe

With God, it's never "Plan B" or
"second best." It's always "Plan A."
And, if we let Him, He'll make something
beautiful of our lives.

Gloria Gaither

When God is involved, anything can
happen. Be open and stay that way.
God has a beautiful way of bringing good
vibrations out of broken chords.

Charles Swindoll

Let your fellowship with the Father and
with the Lord Jesus Christ have as its one
aim and object a life of quiet, determined,
unquestioning obedience.

Andrew Murray

The responsible person seeks to make
his or her whole life a response
to the question and call of God.

Dietrich Bonhoeffer

It ought to be the business of every day
to prepare for our last day.

Matthew Henry

Live in such a way that any day would
make a suitable capstone for life.
Live so that you need not change
your mode of living, even if your sudden
departure were immediately
predicted to you.

C. H. Spurgeon

I'm convinced that there is nothing that
can happen to me in this life that is not
precisely designed by a sovereign Lord
to give me the opportunity to
learn to know Him.

Elisabeth Elliot

Fear not that thy life shall come to an end,
but rather fear that it shall never
have a beginning.

Cardinal Newman

Don't Be
in Such a Hurry

Perhaps you're in a hurry to understand God's unfolding plan for your life. If so, remember that God operates according to a perfect timetable. That timetable is His, not yours. So be patient. God has big things in store for you, but He may have quite a few lessons to teach you *before* you are fully prepared to do His will and fulfill His purpose.

Chapter 2

Where Does God Want Me to Go?

Teach me Your way, O Lord;
I will walk in Your truth.
Psalm 86:11 NKJV

God has things He wants you to do and places He wants you to go. The most important decision of your life is, of course, your commitment to accept Jesus Christ as your personal Lord and Savior. And, once your eternal destiny is secured, you will undoubtedly ask yourself the question "What now, Lord?" If you earnestly seek God's will for your life, you will find it . . . in time.

As you seek to discover God's path for your life, you should study His Holy Word and be ever watchful for His signs. You should associate with fellow Christians who will encourage your spiritual growth, and you should listen to that inner voice that speaks to you in the quiet moments of your daily devotionals.

Rest assured: God is here, and He intends to use you in wonderful, unexpected ways. He desires to lead you along a path of His choosing. Your challenge is to watch, to listen . . . and to follow.

Live out your life
in its full meaning.
It is God's life.

–

Josiah Royce

Unless the Lord builds the house, they labor in vain who build it; unless the Lord guards the city, the watchman stays awake in vain.

Psalm 127:1 NKJV

Their distress is due entirely to their deliberate determination to use themselves for a purpose other than God's.

Oswald Chambers

Aim at Heaven
and you will get earth "thrown in";
aim at earth and you will get neither.

C. S. Lewis

Without God, life has no purpose,
and without purpose, life has no meaning.

Rick Warren

What you get by reaching your goals is not nearly as important as what you become by reaching them.

Zig Ziglar

"I say this because I know what I am planning for you," says the Lord. "I have good plans for you, not plans to hurt you. I will give you hope and a good future."

Jeremiah 29:11 NCV

The value of a life can only be estimated by its relationship to God.

Oswald Chambers

Life is God's novel. Let him write it.

Isaac Bashevis Singer

We honor God by asking for great things
when they are part of His promise.
We dishonor Him and cheat ourselves
when we ask for molehills where
He has offered mountains.

Vance Havner

You were made by God and for God—
and until you understand that,
life will not make sense.

Rick Warren

Life is not a problem to be solved;
it is an adventure to be lived.

John Eldredge

A man's heart plans his way, But the Lord directs his steps.

Proverbs 16:9 NKJV

Trust God's Timing

God has very big plans in store for your life, so trust Him and wait patiently for those plans to unfold. And remember: God's timing is best, so don't allow yourself to become discouraged if things don't work out exactly as you wish. Instead of worrying about your future, entrust it to God. He knows exactly what you need and exactly when you need it.

Chapter 3

Extreme Demands
and
High Expectations

*Our only goal is to please God whether we
live here or there, because we must
all stand before Christ to be judged.*
2 Corinthians 5:9-10 NCV

Expectations, expectations, expectations! As a young adult living in the 21st century, you know that demands can be high, and expectations even higher. The media delivers an endless stream of messages that tell you how to look, how to behave, how to eat, and how to dress. The media's expectations are impossible to meet—God's are not. God doesn't expect you to be perfect . . . and neither should you.

The difference between perfectionism and realistic expectations is the difference between a life of frustration and a life of contentment. Only one earthly being ever lived life to perfection, and He was the Son of God. The rest of us have fallen short of God's standard and need to be accepting of our own limitations as well as the limitations of others.

If you find yourself frustrated by the unrealistic demands of others (or by unrealistic pressures of the self-imposed variety), it's time to ask yourself who you're trying to impress, and why.

If you're trying to impress your friends, or if you're trying to imitate the appearance of some rail-thin Hollywood celebrity, it's time to reconsider your priorities. Your first responsibility is to the Heavenly Father who created you and to the Son who saved you. Then, you bear a powerful responsibility to be true *to yourself*. And of course you owe debts of gratitude to friends and family members. But, when it comes to meeting society's unrealistic expectations, forget it!

If you become discouraged with your inability to be perfect, remember that when you accepted Christ as your Savior, God accepted you for all eternity. Now, it's your turn to accept *yourself*. When you do, you'll feel a tremendous weight being lifted from your shoulders. After all, pleasing God is simply a matter of obeying His commandments and accepting His Son. But as for pleasing everybody else? *That's* impossible!

If you try to be everything to everybody,
you will end up being nothing to anybody.

Vance Havner

If you just set out to be liked, you would be
prepared to compromise on anything at
any time, and you would achieve nothing.

Margaret Thatcher

Great tranquility has he who cares
neither for praise nor criticism.

Thomas á Kempis

Applause is the spur of noble minds,
the end and aim of weak ones.

Charles Caleb Colton

Pride opens the door to every other sin,
for once we are more concerned with
our reputation than our character,
there is no end to the things
we will do just to make ourselves
"look good" before others.

Warren Wiersbe

True friends will always lift you higher
and challenge you to walk
in a manner pleasing to our Lord.

Lisa Bevere

When we are set free from the bondage
of pleasing others, when we are free from
currying others' favor and others' approval—
then no one will be able to make us
miserable or dissatisfied. And then,
if we know we have pleased God,
contentment will be our consolation.

Kay Arthur

What I must do is all that concerns me,
not what people think.

Ralph Waldo Emerson

Every day, I find countless opportunities
to decide whether I will obey God and
demonstrate my love for Him or try to
please myself or the world system.
God is waiting for my choices.

Bill Bright

Perfectionism 101

Here's what you need to know about perfectionism: it's unrealistic, it's counterproductive, it's habit-forming, and it's dumb. Of course, you should expect excellence from others and from yourself. But, if you allow yourself to become a world-class nitpicker, you're setting yourself up for a lifetime of frustration and disappointment.

In heaven, we will know perfection. Here on earth, we have a few short years to wrestle with the challenges of imperfection. God is perfect; we human beings are not. May we live—and forgive—accordingly.

Chapter 4

A Daily Journey of Prayer and Meditation

*Speak, Lord. I am your servant
and I am listening.*
1 Samuel 3:10 NCV

Once you finally discover God's purpose for your life, your search will be over and your life will be complete . . . right? Wrong! Your search to discover the unfolding of God's plan for your life is not a destination to be reached; it is a path to be traveled, a journey that unfolds day by day. And, that's exactly how often you should seek direction from your Creator: one day at a time, each day followed by the next, without exception.

Daily prayer and meditation is a matter of will and habit. You must willingly organize your time by carving out quiet moments with God, and you must form the habit of daily worship. When you do, you'll discover that no time is more precious than the silent moments you spend with your Heavenly Father.

God promises that the prayers of righteous people can accomplish great things. God promises that He answers prayer (although *His* answers are not always in accordance with *our* desires). God invites us to be still and to feel His presence. So pray. Pray about matters great and small; and be watchful for the answers that God most assuredly sends your way.

Is prayer an integral part of your daily life, or is it a hit-or-miss routine? Do you "pray without ceasing," or do you simply cease praying? Do you pray throughout the day, or do you bow your head only when others are watching?

The quality of your spiritual life will be in direct proportion to the quality of your prayer life. Prayer changes things, and it changes you. Today, instead of turning things over in your mind, turn them over to God in prayer. Instead of worrying about your next decision, ask God to lead the way. Don't limit your prayers to meals or to bedtime; pray constantly. God is listening; He wants to hear from you; and *you* most certainly need to hear from Him.

The life of faith is a daily exploration
of the constant and countless ways in which
God's grace and love are experienced.

Eugene Peterson

When we pray, we have linked ourselves
with Divine purposes, and we therefore
have Divine power at our disposal
for human living.

E. Stanley Jones

We all need to make time for God.
Even Jesus made time
to be alone with the Father.

Kay Arthur

Pour out your heart to God and tell Him
how you feel. Be real, be honest,
and when you get it all out, you'll start
to feel the gradual covering of
God's comforting presence.

Bill Hybels

Don't be overwhelmed . . .
take it one day and one prayer at a time.

Stormie Omartian

History has been changed time after time
because of prayer. I tell you, history could be
changed again if people went
to their knees in believing prayer.

Billy Graham

God shapes the world by prayer.
The more praying there is in the world,
the better the world will be,
and the mightier will be
the forces against evil.

E. M. Bounds

The only way to pray is to pray;
and the way to pray well is to pray much.

Henri Nouwen

Prayer connects us with
God's limitless potential.

Henry Blackaby

Some people pray just to pray,
and some people pray to know God.

Andrew Murray

It is in a prayer relationship that
God gives further direction.

Henry Blackaby and Claude King

If you lack knowledge, go to school.
If you lack wisdom, get on your knees.

Vance Havner

Maintenance of the devotional mood
is indispensable to success
in the Christian life.

A. W. Tozer

Never say you will pray about a thing;
pray about it.

Oswald Chambers

Prayer is never the least we can do;
it is always the most!

A. W. Tozer

*Ask and it will be given to you;
seek and you will find; knock and the door
will be opened to you. For everyone who
asks receives; he who seeks finds; and to him
who knocks, the door will be opened.*

Matthew 7:7-8 NKJV

On our knees we are the most powerful
force on earth.

Billy Graham

If you want to hear God's voice clearly and
you are uncertain, then remain
in His presence until He changes that
uncertainty. Often, much can happen
during this waiting for the Lord.
Sometimes, he changes pride into humility,
doubt into faith and peace.

Corrie ten Boom

When you meet with God, open the Bible.
Don't rely on your memory;
rely on those printed pages.

Charles Swindoll

Prayer shouldn't be casual or sporadic,
dictated only by the needs of the moment.
Prayer should be as much a part
of our lives as breathing.

Billy Graham

Prayer keeps us in constant communion
with God, which is the goal
of our entire believing lives.

Beth Moore

The remedy for distractions is the same now
as it was in earlier and simpler times:
prayer, meditation, and the cultivation
of the inner life.

A. W. Tozer

He awakens me morning by morning,
He awakens my ear to hear as the learned.

Isaiah 50:4 NKJV

Rejoice always, pray without ceasing,
in everything give thanks; for this is the will
of God in Christ Jesus for you.

1 Thessalonians 5:16-18 NKJV

To pray is to mount on eagle's wings above
the clouds and get into the clear heaven
where God dwells.

C. H. Spurgeon

Spending a Few Minutes Each Day with God

Okay, you're busy . . . *very* busy. But you're *not* too busy to spend a few minutes each day with God. Scottish-born evangelist Henry Drummond correctly observed, "Ten minutes spent in Christ's company every day—even two minutes—will make the whole day different." How true. If you dedicate even a few minutes each morning to a time of devotional reading and prayer, you will change the tone and direction of your life.

If you're staying up late and sleeping through the early morning hours, perhaps it's time to rearrange your schedule. And, if you're staying up in order to watch one more late-night rerun, do yourself a favor: go to bed. As Ben Franklin correctly observed, "The early morning is golden."

Chapter 5

Trusting
God's Direction

Whoever listens to what is taught will succeed,
and whoever trusts the Lord will be happy.
Proverbs 16:20 NCV

God has things He wants to tell us, and He's hard at work trying to get His message through; unfortunately, many of us are too busy, too distracted, or too stubborn to listen. So instead of discovering God's direction, we may wander around, searching for abundance and happiness, but never finding it.

If you choose to wander aimlessly through this life, nobody can stop you. But if you sincerely seek to discover God's purpose (and experience His abundance), here are seven things that you can do.

1. Carve out time for daily prayer, meditation, and Bible study: even a few minutes each day can make a big difference in your life.

2. Attend worship services regularly and be a contributing member of your fellowship: fellow Christians will help you become a better Christian.

3. Choose friends who encourage you to do the right thing (and while you're at it, avoid people who tempt you to do otherwise).

4. Seek the wisdom of mentors, trusted friends, and family members (and don't be too stubborn to accept their advice).

5. Be watchful for signs: remember that sometimes God's messages are subtle.

6. Listen to your conscience, and pay attention to the quiet voice that speaks to you when you genuinely open your heart to God.

7. If at first you don't succeed, don't allow yourself to become discouraged. Instead, keep trusting God and keep seeking His direction until you find it . . . and rest assured: you *will* find it.

Let not your heart be troubled;
you believe in God, believe also in Me.

John 14:1 NKJV

This whole matter of Christian living is
simply one issue: believing God.

Vance Havner

Never imagine that you can be a loser
by trusting in God.

C. H. Spurgeon

Trust in yourself and you are doomed
to disappointment; trust in money
and you may have it taken from you,
but trust in God, and you are never to be
confounded in time or eternity.

D. L. Moody

Walk by faith! Stop the plague of worry.
Relax! Learn to say,
"Lord, this is Your battle."

Charles Swindoll

We shall steer safely through every storm,
as long as our heart is right, our intention
fervent, our courage steadfast,
and our trust fixed in God.

St. Francis de Sales

Confidence in the natural world is
self-reliance; in the spiritual world,
it is God-reliance.

Oswald Chambers

God is God. He knows what he is doing.
When you can't trace his hand,
trust his heart.

Max Lucado

What is needed is not the removal
of trouble but the conquest of self.

C. H. Spurgeon

Trust the past to God's mercy,
the present to God's love,
and the future to God's providence.

St. Augustine

We cannot rely on God's promises without
obeying his commandments.

John Calvin

Are you serious about wanting
God's guidance to become the person
he wants you to be? The first step is to tell
God that you know you can't manage
your own life; that you need his help.

Catherine Marshall

Never be afraid to trust an unknown future
to a known God.

Corrie ten Boom

Never place a period
where God
has placed a comma.

Mother Teresa

Trust the Father

Are you tired? Discouraged? Fearful? Be comforted and trust God. Are you worried or anxious? Be confident in God's power. He will never desert you. Do you see no hope for the future? Be courageous and call upon God. He will protect you and then use you according to His purposes. Are you grieving? Know that God hears your suffering. He will comfort you and, in time, He will heal you. Are you confused? Listen to the quiet voice of your Heavenly Father. He is not a God of confusion. Talk with Him; listen to Him; trust Him. He is steadfast, and He is your Protector . . . forever.

Chapter 6

Choosing Your Friends, Choosing Your Behaviors

As iron sharpens iron,
so people can improve each other.
Proverbs 27:17 NCV

S ome friendships help us honor God; these friendships should be nurtured. Other friendships place us in situations where we are tempted to dishonor God by disobeying His commandments; friendships that dishonor God have the potential to do us great harm.

Because we tend to become like our friends, we must choose our friends carefully. Because our friends influence us in ways that are both subtle and powerful, we must ensure that our friendships are pleasing to God. When we spend our days in the presence of godly believers, we are blessed, not only by those friends, but also by our Creator.

Do you seek to live a life that is pleasing to God? If so, you should build friendships that are pleasing to Him. When you do, your Heavenly Father will bless you and your friends with gifts that are simply too numerous to count.

If you choose to awaken
a passion for God, you will
have to choose your friends wisely.

Lisa Bevere

Do you want to be wise?
Choose wise friends.

Charles Swindoll

Tell me what company you keep,
and I'll tell you what you are.

Miguel de Cervantes

For better or worse, you will eventually
become more and more like the people you
associate with. So why not associate with
people who make you better, not worse?

Marie T. Freeman

The simple fact is that if we sow
a lifestyle that is in direct disobedience
to God's revealed Word,
we ultimately reap disaster.

Charles Swindoll

Don't worry about what you do not
understand. Worry about what you do
understand in the Bible but do not live by.

Corrie ten Boom

Our walk counts far more
than our talk, always!

George Mueller

Your life together with other believers
stands as the best confirmation
that you know God.

Stanley Grenz

What you do reveals what you believe
about God, regardless of what you say.
When God reveals what He has purposed
to do, you face a crisis—a decision time.
God and the world can tell from
your response what you
really believe about God.

Henry Blackaby

Morality and immorality are not defined
by man's changing attitudes and social
customs. They are determined by the God
of the universe, whose timeless standards
cannot be ignored with impunity.

James Dobson

We can always gauge where we are
by the teachings of Jesus Christ.

Oswald Chambers

We are to leave an impression on all those
we meet that communicates whose we are
and what kingdom we represent.

Lisa Bevere

Peer Pressure 101

Here's what you need to know about peer pressure:

1. Peer pressure exists, and you will experience it.
2. If your peers encourage you to behave yourself, to honor God, and to become a better person, peer pressure can actually be a good thing . . . up to a point. But remember: you don't have to be perfect to be wonderful. So if you're trying to be perfect, lighten up on yourself, and while you're at it, lighten up on others, too.
3. If your friends are encouraging you to misbehave or underachieve, find new friends. Today.

Chapter 7

Discovering
the Power of Faith

If you have faith as a mustard seed,
you will say to this mountain,
"Move from here to there," and it will move;
and nothing will be impossible for you.
Matthew 17:20 NKJV

Jesus taught His disciples that if they had faith, they could move mountains. You can too.

When a suffering woman sought healing by merely touching the hem of His cloak, Jesus replied, "Be of good cheer, daughter; your faith has made you well" (Matthew 9:22 NKJV). The message to believers of every generation is clear: we must live by faith today and every day.

When you place your faith, your trust, indeed your life in the hands of Christ Jesus, you'll be amazed at the marvelous things He can do with you and through you. So strengthen your faith through praise, through worship, through Bible study, and through prayer. And trust God's plans. With Him, all things are possible, and He stands ready to open a world of possibilities to you . . . if you have faith.

Fear is a self-imposed prison that will
keep you from becoming what
God intends for you to be.

Rick Warren

Fear lurks in the shadows
of every area of life.
The future may look very threatening.
Jesus says, "Stop being afraid. Trust me!"

Charles Swindoll

God alone can give us songs in the night.

C. H. Spurgeon

Earthly fears are no fears at all.
Answer the big question of eternity,
and the little questions of life fall
into perspective.

Max Lucado

Do not build up
obstacles in your
imagination.
Difficulties must be
studied and dealt with,
but they must not be
magnified by fear.

Norman Vincent Peale

In the spiritual life, whoever doesn't
go forward goes backward.
It's the same with a boat that must
always go forward. If it stands still,
the wind will blow it back.

Padre Pio of Pietrelcina

The great paralysis of our heart is unbelief.

Oswald Chambers

When you ask God to do something,
don't ask timidly;
put your whole heart into it.

Marie T. Freeman

Be patient. When you feel lonely,
stay with your loneliness. Avoid the
temptation to let your fearful self run off.
Let it teach you its wisdom; let it tell you
that you can live instead of just surviving.
Gradually you will become one, and you will
find that Jesus is living in your heart and
offering you all you need.

Henri Nouwen

There comes a time when we simply have
to face the challenges in our lives
and stop backing down.

John Eldredge

No one is surprised over what
God does when he has faith in Him.

Oswald Chambers

Faith is two empty hands held open
to receive all of the Lord Jesus.

Alan Redpath

Faith means believing in advance
what will only make sense in reverse.

Philip Yancey

Faith in God will not get for you everything
you want, but it will get for you what
God wants you to have. The unbeliever
does not need what he wants; the Christian
should want only what he needs.

Vance Havner

*Blessed is the man whose strength is in You,
whose heart is set on pilgrimage.*

Psalm 84:5 NKJV

Only God can move mountains,
but faith and prayer can move God.

E. M. Bounds

*Jesus said to him, "If you can believe,
all things are possible to him who believes."*

Mark 9:23 NKJV

Faith is the belief that
God will do what is right.

Max Lucado

Trust God
and Get Busy

Here's a time-tested formula for success: have faith in God and do the work. Hard work is not simply a proven way to get ahead; it's also part of God's plan for you. God did not create you for a life of mediocrity; He created you for far greater things. Reaching for greater things usually requires work and lots of it, which is perfectly fine with God. After all, He knows that you're up to the task, and He has big plans for you if you possess a loving heart and willing hands.

Chapter 8

Discovering the Power of Optimism

I can do all things through
Christ who strengthens me.
Philippians 4:13 NKJV

Are you an optimistic, hopeful, enthusiastic Christian? You should be. After all, as a believer, you have every reason to be optimistic about life here on earth and life eternal. As C. H. Spurgeon observed, "Our hope in Christ for the future is the mainstream of our joy." But sometimes, you may find yourself pulled down by the inevitable demands and worries of life-here-on-earth. If you find yourself discouraged, exhausted, or both, then it's time to take your concerns to God. When you do, He will lift your spirits and renew your strength.

Today, make this promise to yourself and keep it: vow to be a hope-filled Christian. Think optimistically about your life, your friends, your family, and your future. Trust your hopes, not your fears. Take time to celebrate God's glorious creation. And then, when you've filled your heart with hope and gladness, share your optimism with others. They'll be better for it, and so will you.

The things we think are the things that
feed our souls. If we think on pure
and lovely things, we shall grow pure
and lovely like them;
and the converse is equally true.

Hannah Whitall Smith

No pessimist ever discovered the secrets
of the stars or sailed to an uncharted land,
or opened a new heaven
to the human spirit.

Helen Keller

The people whom I have seen succeed best
in life have always been cheerful and hopeful
people who went about their business
with a smile on their faces.

Charles Kingsley

It is not fitting, when one is in
God's service, to have a gloomy face
or a chilling look.

St. Francis of Assisi

Remember always that there are two things
which are more utterly incompatible
even than oil and water,
and these two are trust and worry.

Hannah Whitall Smith

We can accomplish almost anything within
our ability if we but think we can.

George Matthew Adams

The essence of optimism is that it takes no
account of the present, but it is a source of
inspiration, of vitality, and of hope. Where
others have resigned, it enables a man to
hold his head high, to claim the future for
himself, and not abandon it to his enemy.

Dietrich Bonhoeffer

We are either the masters or the victims
of our attitudes. It is a matter of personal
choice. Who we are today is the result of
choices we made yesterday. Tomorrow, we
will become what we choose today.
To change means to choose to change.

John Maxwell

We must admit that we spend more of our
time concentrating and fretting over the
things that can't be changed than we do
giving attention to the one thing we can
change: our choice of attitude.

Charles Swindoll

The life of strain is difficult.
The life of inner peace—
a life that comes from a positive attitude—
is the easiest type of existence.

Norman Vincent Peale

He who believes is strong;
he who doubts is weak.
Strong convictions precede great actions.

James Freeman Clarke

Outlook determines outcome
and attitude determines action.

Warren Wiersbe

Perpetual optimism is a force multiplier.

Colin Powell

Change your thoughts,
and you change your world.

Norman Vincent Peale

Be anxious for nothing, but in everything
by prayer and supplication, with thanksgiving,
let your requests be made known to God.

Philippians 4:6 NKJV

Worry and anxiety are sand
in the machinery of life; faith is the oil.

E. Stanley Jones

We know so little about the future
that to worry about it would be
the height of foolishness.

C. H. Spurgeon

By the anxieties and worries of this life
Satan tries to dull man's heart and
make a dwelling for himself there.

St. Francis of Assisi

Often, attitude is the only difference
between success and failure.

John Maxwell

The beginning of anxiety is the end of faith,
and the beginning of true faith
is the end of anxiety.

George Mueller

The fierce grip of panic need not
immobilize you. God knows no limitation
when it comes to deliverance.
Admit your fear. Commit it to Him.
Dump the pressure on Him.
He can handle it.

Charles Swindoll

Do you wonder where you can go
for encouragement and motivation?
Run to Jesus.

Max Lucado

Putting the Self-fulfilling Prophecy to Work for You

As you plan for your future, be aware that attitudes have a way of transforming themselves into reality. In other words, *how* you think will help determine *what* you become. So think realistically about yourself and your situation while making a conscious effort to focus on hopes, not fears. When you do, you'll put the self-fulfilling prophecy to work for you.

Chapter 9

Becoming
Your Own Person

*But grow in the grace and knowledge
of our Lord and Savior Jesus Christ.
To Him be the glory both now and forever.*
2 Peter 3:18 NKJV

When God made you, He equipped you with an assortment of talents and abilities that are uniquely yours. It's up to you to discover those talents and to use them, but sometimes the world will encourage you to do otherwise. At times, our society will attempt to cubbyhole you, to standardize you, and to make you fit into a particular, preformed mold. Perhaps God has other plans.

Have you found something in this life that you're passionate about? Something that inspires you to jump out of bed in the morning and hit the ground running? And does your work honor the Creator by making His world a better place? If so, congratulations: you're using your gifts well.

Sometimes, because you're a fallible human being, you may become so wrapped up in meeting *society's* expectations that you fail to focus on *God's* expectations. To do so is a mistake of major proportions—don't make it. Instead, seek God's guidance as you focus your energies on becoming the best "you" that you can possibly be.

What's the best way to thank God for the gifts that He has given you? By using them. And you might as well start using them today.

———

Our souls were made to live in
an upper atmosphere, and we stifle and
choke if we live on any lower level.
Our eyes were made to look off from these
heavenly heights, and our vision is
distorted by any lower gazing.

Hannah Whitall Smith

As each one has received a gift,
minister it to one another,
as good stewards of the manifold grace of God.

1 Peter 4:10 NKJV

We must make the choices that enable us
to fulfill the deepest capacities
of our real selves.

Thomas Merton

It is certain that man never achieves
a clear knowledge of himself unless
he has first looked upon God's face,
and then descends from contemplating him
to scrutinize himself.

John Calvin

O God. You are always the same.
Let me know myself and know You.

St. Augustine

When one is estranged from oneself,
then one is estranged from others, too.

Anne Morrow Lindbergh

Develop a style that suits you, and pursue it.
Always be yourself.

Jimmy Stewart

Don't wish to be anything but what you are,
and try to be that perfectly.

St. Francis of Sales

Converting Talent into Skill Requires Work

God gives us talents for a reason: to use them. Each of us possesses special abilities, gifted by God, that can be nurtured carefully or ignored totally. Our challenge, of course, is to use our talents to the greatest extent possible. But we are mightily tempted to do otherwise. Why? Because converting raw talent into polished skill usually requires work, and lots of it.

God's Word clearly instructs us to do the hard work of refining our talents for the glory of His kingdom and the service of His people. So, we are wise to remember the old adage: "What we are is God's gift to us; what we become is our gift to God." May we work diligently to ensure that our gifts are worthy of the Giver.

Chapter 10

Praying *on* Purpose *for* Purpose

Ask and it will be given to you;
seek and you will find;
knock and the door will be opened to you.
For everyone who asks receives;
he who seeks finds; and to him who knocks,
the door will be opened.
Matthew 7:7-8 NKJV

J esus made it clear to His disciples: they should pray always. So should we. Genuine, heartfelt prayer produces powerful changes in us *and* in our world. When we lift our hearts to our Father in heaven, we open ourselves to a never-ending source of divine wisdom and infinite love.

Have you fervently asked God for His guidance in every aspect of your life? If so, then you're continually inviting your Creator to reveal Himself in a variety of ways. As a follower of Christ, you must do no less.

Do you have questions about your future that you simply can't answer? Ask for the guidance of your Heavenly Father. Do you sincerely seek to know God's purpose for your life? Then ask Him for direction—and *keep* asking Him every day that you live. Whatever your need, no matter how great or small, pray about it and never lose hope. God is not just near; He is here, and He's ready to talk with you. Now!

It is in a prayer relationship that
God gives further direction.

Henry Blackaby and Claude King

If you lack knowledge, go to school.
If you lack wisdom, get on your knees.

Vance Havner

Prayer is not a lovely sedan for a sightseeing
trip around the city. Prayer is a truck that
goes straight to the warehouse, backs up,
loads, and comes home with the goods.

John R. Rice

Prayer plumes the wings of God's young
eaglets so that they may learn to mount
above the clouds. Prayer brings inner
strength to God's warriors and sends them
forth to spiritual battle with their muscles
firm and their armor in place.

C. H. Spurgeon

There will be no power in our lives
apart from prayer.

Angela Thomas

Prayer is never the least we can do;
it is always the most!

A. W. Tozer

Prayer shouldn't be casual or sporadic,
dictated only by the needs of the moment.
Prayer should be as much a part
of our lives as breathing.

Billy Graham

Never say you will pray about a thing;
pray about it.

Oswald Chambers

If God, like a father, denies us what we want
now, it is in order to give us some far better
thing later on. The will of God, we can
rest assured, is invariably a better thing.

Elisabeth Elliot

Rejoice always, pray without ceasing,
in everything give thanks;
for this is the will of God in Christ Jesus for you.
1 Thessalonians 5:16-18 NKJV

If the spiritual life is to be healthy
and under the full power of the Holy Spirit,
praying without ceasing will be natural.

Andrew Murray

May He grant you according to
your heart's desire, and fulfill all your purpose.
Psalm 20:4 NKJV

Sometimes, the Answer Is "No"

God does not answer all of our prayers in the affirmative, nor should He. His job is not to grant all our earthly requests; His job is to offer us eternal salvation (for which we must be eternally grateful).

When we are disappointed by the realities of life-here-on-earth, we should remember that our prayers are always answered by a sovereign, all-knowing God, and that we must trust Him, whether He answers "Yes," "No," or "Not yet."

Chapter 11

Changes, Changes, and More Changes

*To everything there is a season,
a time for every purpose under heaven.*
Ecclesiastes 3:1 NKJV

Our world is in a state of constant change; God is not. At times, everything around us seems to be changing: our relationships change; we grow older; loved ones die. Sometimes, the world seems to be trembling beneath our feet. But we can be comforted in the knowledge that our Heavenly Father is the rock that cannot be shaken. His Word promises, "I am the Lord, I do not change" (Malachi 3:6 NKJV).

Every day that we live, we mortals encounter a multitude of changes—some good, some not so good. And on occasion, all of us must endure life-changing personal losses that leave us breathless. When we do, our loving Heavenly Father stands ready to protect us, to comfort us, to guide us, and, in time, to heal us.

Are you facing difficult transitions or unwelcome adjustments? If so, please remember that God is far bigger than any challenge you may face. So, instead of worrying about the shifting sands of life, put your faith in the One who cannot be moved.

Are you anxious about situations that you cannot control? Take your anxieties to God. Are you troubled? Take your troubles to Him. Does your world seem to be changing too fast for its own good? Remember that "Jesus Christ is the same yesterday, today, and forever" (Hebrews 13:8 NKJV). And, rest assured: It is precisely because your Savior does not change that you can face the transitions of life with courage for today and hope for tomorrow.

———

Never be afraid to trust an unknown future to an all-knowing God.

Corrie ten Boom

Let nothing disturb you,
nothing frighten you; all things are passing;
God never changes.

St. Teresa of Avila

The maturity of a Christian experience
cannot be reached in a moment, but is the
result of the work of God's Holy Spirit, who,
by His energizing and transforming power,
causes us to grow up into
Christ in all things.

Hannah Whitall Smith

Often, in the midst of great problems,
we stop short of the real blessing
God has for us,
which is a fresh vision of who He is.

Anne Graham Lotz

Today is not yesterday. We ourselves change.
How can our works and thoughts,
if they are always to be the fittest, continue
always the same? Change, indeed, is painful,
yet ever needful; and if memory has its force
and worth, so also has hope.

Thomas Carlyle

Pain is inevitable, but misery is optional.

Max Lucado

It is well and good if all things change,
Lord, if we are rooted in You.

St. John of the Cross

Ask the God who made you
to keep remaking you.
Norman Vincent Peale

Change Is Inevitable; Growth Is Not

The world keeps changing, and so, hopefully, do we. We are mightily tempted to remain stagnant (we perceive that it's safer "here" than "there"). But God has bigger plans for us. He intends that we continue to mature throughout every stage of life. Toward that end, God comes to our doorsteps with countless opportunities to learn and to grow. And He knocks. Our challenge, of course, is to open the door.

Chapter 12

Doing Your Work, Discovering Your Mission

And whatever you do,
do it heartily, as to the Lord and not to men.
Colossians 3:23 NKJV

God has work for you to do, but He won't make you do it. Ever since the days of Adam and Eve, God has allowed His children to make choices for themselves, and so it is with you. You've got choices to make . . . lots of them. If you choose wisely, you'll be rewarded; if you choose unwisely, you'll bear the consequences.

Whether you're in school or in the workplace, your success will depend, in large part, upon the quality and quantity of your work. God has created a world in which diligence is rewarded and sloth is not. So whatever you choose to do, do it with commitment, excitement, and vigor.

God did not create you for a life of mediocrity; He created you for far greater things. Reaching for greater things usually requires work and lots of it, which is perfectly fine with God. After all, He knows that you're up to the task, and He has big plans for you. Very big plans . . .

Only God's chosen task for you will
ultimately satisfy. Do not wait until it is too
late to realize the privilege of serving Him in
His chosen position for you.

Beth Moore

Christians are to "labor," which refers to
hard, manual work. Hard work is honorable.
As Christians we should work hard
so that we will have enough to give
to those in need, not so that we will have
more of what we don't need.

John MacArthur

Whatever your hand finds to do,
do it with your might.

Ecclesiastes 9:10 NKJV

Know thy work and do it.

Thomas Carlyle

Think enthusiastically about everything,
especially your work.

Norman Vincent Peale

What a great prize it is:
the chance to work hard
at work worth doing.

Theodore Roosevelt

Can anything be sadder than work unfinished? Yes: work never begun.

–

Christina Rossetti

Each man has his own vocation;
his talent is his call. There is one direction
in which all space is open to him.

Ralph Waldo Emerson

I seem to have been led, little by little,
toward my work; and I believe that the same
fact will appear in the life of anyone who
will cultivate such powers as God has given
him and then go on, bravely, quietly,
but persistently, doing such work
as comes to his hands.

Fanny Crosby

The world does not consider labor
a blessing, therefore it flees and hates it,
but the pious who fear the Lord labor
with a ready and cheerful heart,
for they know God's command,
and they acknowledge His calling.

Martin Luther

The best preparation for tomorrow is to do
today's work superbly well.

William Osler

You will always have joy in the evening
if you spend the day fruitfully.

Thomas à Kempis

Faith and work make
a triumphant combination.

Father Flanagan

Work joyfully and peacefully, knowing that
right thoughts and right efforts will
inevitably bring about right results.

James Allen

Get absolutely enthralled with something.
Throw yourself into it with abandon.
Get out of yourself. Be somebody.
Do something.

Norman Vincent Peale

Consider every day that you are
then for the first time—as it were—beginning;
and always act with the same fervour
as on the first day you began.

Anthony of Padua

Don't take hold of a thing unless you want
that thing to take hold of you.

E. Stanley Jones

Everything worthwhile,
everything of any value, has a price.
The price is effort.

Loretta Young

The key to success?
Understanding that there's no free lunch.

Lou Holtz

Be like a postage stamp:
stick to one thing till you get there.

Josh Billings

Nothing will work unless you do.

John Wooden

One Career or Many?

Only a generation or two ago, men and women entered the workplace with the expectation that one career might last a lifetime. For most of us, those days are gone, probably forever. Today, our world is changing more rapidly than ever before, and so is the job market. In response, you'll need to keep expanding your skills and keep looking for new opportunities. So keep learning, keep networking, and keep your eyes open for the next big thing . . . it's probably just around the corner.

Chapter 13

Purposeful Worship, Purposeful Praise

All the earth shall worship You
And sing praises to You;
They shall sing praises to Your name.
Psalm 66:4 NKJV

All of humanity is engaged in worship. The question is not *whether* we worship, but *what* we worship. Wise men and women choose to worship God. When they do, they are blessed with a plentiful harvest of joy, peace, and abundance. Other people choose to distance themselves from God by foolishly worshiping things that are intended to bring *personal* gratification, not *spiritual* gratification. Such choices often have tragic consequences.

If we place our love for material possessions above our love for God—or if we yield to the countless temptations of this world—we find ourselves engaged in a struggle between good and evil, a clash between God and Satan. Our responses to these struggles have implications that echo throughout our families and throughout our communities.

How can we ensure that we cast our lot with God? We do so, in part, by the practice of regular, purposeful worship in the company of fellow believers. When we worship God faithfully and fervently, we are blessed. When we fail to worship God, for whatever reason, we forfeit the spiritual gifts that He intends for us.

We must worship our Heavenly Father, not just with our words, but also with deeds. We must honor Him, praise Him, and obey Him. As we seek to find purpose and meaning for our lives, we must first seek *His* purpose and *His* will. For believers, God comes first. Always first.

———

The Creator loves you very much since
He gives you so many good things.
Therefore, be careful not to be ungrateful,
but strive always to praise God.

St. Francis of Assisi

It is impossible to worship God
and remain unchanged.

Henry Blackaby

It may take a lifetime to learn to focus
on God, to pull our gaze off the world,
off ourselves, off our goals, and to fully
gaze on him and worship him.

Mary Morrison Suggs

The deepest level of worship is praising God
in spite of pain, thanking God during a trial,
trusting him when tempted, surrendering
while suffering, and loving him when
he seems distant.

Rick Warren

Praise and thank God for who He is
and for what He has done for you.

Billy Graham

Worship is a voluntary act of gratitude
offered by the saved to the Savior,
by the healed to the Healer,
by the delivered to the Deliverer.

Max Lucado

Each time, before you intercede, be quiet
first and worship God in His glory.
Think of what He can do and how He
delights to hear the prayers of His redeemed
people. Think of your place and privilege in
Christ, and expect great things!

Andrew Murray

The fact that we were created to enjoy God
and to worship him forever
is etched upon our souls.

Jim Cymbala

God being who He is must always
be sought for Himself,
never as a means toward something else.

A. W. Tozer

Worship is a lifestyle.

Joey Johnson

To praise God is to please God.

Jim Gallery

It is only with gratitude that life becomes rich.

Dietrich Bonhoeffer

God asks that we worship Him
with our concentrated minds as well as
with our wills and emotions. A divided and
scattered mind is not effective.

Catherine Marshall

Our God is the sovereign Creator of
the universe! He loves us as His own
children and has provided every
good thing we have; He is worthy of
our praise every moment.

Shirley Dobson

Be not afraid of saying too much
in the praises of God; all the danger
is of saying too little.

Matthew Henry

The Bible instructs—and experience
teaches—that praising God results
in our burdens being lifted
and our joys being multiplied.

Jim Gallery

Praise reestablishes the proper chain of
command; we recognize that the King
is on the throne and that
he has saved his people.

Max Lucado

Holy, holy, holy! Lord God Almighty!
All Thy works shall praise Thy name
in earth, and sky, and sea.

Reginald Heber

Knowing a God who is
holy and compassionate
ought to lead to joyful
and awe-filled praise
to this glorious God.

–

Stanley Grenz

When there is peace in the heart,
there will be praise on the lips.

Warren Wiersbe

Don't ever come to church without coming
as though it were the first time,
as though it could be the best time,
and as though it might be the last time.

Vance Havner

The time for universal praise is
sure to come some day.
Let us begin to do our part now.

Hannah Whitall Smith

Sunday Morning Only or 24/7?

Worship is not meant to be boxed up in a church building on Sunday morning. To the contrary, praise and worship should be woven into the very fabric of our lives.

Do you take time each day to worship your Father in heaven, or do you wait until Sunday morning to praise Him for His blessings? The answer to this question will, in large part, determine the quality and direction of your life. So worship accordingly.

Chapter 14

Watching for Signs

*Blessed are those servants whom the master,
when he comes, will find watching.*
Luke 12:37 NKJV

G od has plans for your life, but He won't force those plans upon you. To the contrary, He has given you free will, the ability to make decisions on your own. With that freedom to choose comes the responsibility of living with the consequences of the choices you make.

If you seek to live in accordance with God's will for your life—and you should—then you will contemplate His Word, and you will be watchful for His signs. You will associate with fellow Christians who will encourage your spiritual growth, and you will listen to that inner voice that speaks to you in the quiet moments of your daily devotionals.

God intends to use you in wonderful, unexpected ways if you let Him, but be forewarned: the decision to seek God's plan and fulfill His purpose is yours and yours alone. The consequences of that decision have implications that are both profound and eternal, so choose carefully. And, as you go about your daily activities, keep your eyes and ears open . . . as well as your heart.

Blessed are those who hunger and thirst for
righteousness, For they shall be filled.

Matthew 5:6 NKJV

Mark it down. God never turns away
the honest seeker. Go to God with
your questions. You may not find
all the answers, but in finding God,
you know the One who does.

Max Lucado

God is a place of safety you can run to,
but it helps if you are running to Him
on a daily basis so that you are
in familiar territory.

Stormie Omartian

You will be able to trust Him
only to the extent that you know Him!

Kay Arthur

The Wisdom of Silence

We live in a very noisy world. We are bombarded with instant messages, booming music, and unlimited information. Perhaps you've allowed this noise to fill every waking moment of your life, or perhaps you've allowed it to interfere with those quiet moments when God might otherwise speak to your heart. If so, it's time to click off the radio, the television, the computer, and the cell phone—for awhile.

Try this experiment: the next time you're alone spend that time without a radio, CDs, or a cell phone. And then, have a quiet talk with God about His plans for your life. You may be surprised to discover that sometimes the most important answers are the ones you receive in silence.

Chapter 15

And Finally . . .

I have come that they may have life,
and that they may have it more abundantly.
John 10:10 NKJV

We conclude with a few words of wisdom about God's blessings. May you discover His will, and may you experience His love today and forever.

Do we not continually pass by blessings innumerable without notice, and instead fix our eyes on what we feel to be our trials and our losses, and think and talk about these until our whole horizon is filled with them, and we almost begin to think we have no blessings at all?

Hannah Whitall Smith

Jesus intended for us to be overwhelmed by the blessings of regular days.

Gloria Gaither

The Bible says that being a Christian is not only a great way to die, but it's also the best way to live.

Bill Hybels

God loves you and wants you to experience peace and life-abundant and eternal.

–

Billy Graham

God does not give us everything we want,
but He does fulfill all His promises
as He leads us along the best
and straightest paths to Himself.

Dietrich Bonhoeffer

If all struggles and sufferings were
eliminated, the spirit would no more reach
maturity than would the child.

Elisabeth Elliot

True moral freedom is the ability
to live according to God's purposes.

Stanley Grenz

God cannot lead the individual who
is not willing to give Him
a blank check with his life.

Catherine Marshall

Our heavenly Father
never takes anything
from his children
unless he means to
give them something
better.

-

George Mueller

Do not limit the limitless God!
With Him, face the future unafraid
because you are never alone.

Mrs. Charles E. Cowman

**Think of the blessings we so easily take
for granted:** Life itself; preservation from
danger; every bit of health we enjoy; every
hour of liberty; the ability to see, to hear,
to speak, to think, and to imagine all this
comes from the hand of God.

We do not need to beg Him to bless us;
He simply cannot help it.

Hannah Whitall Smith

We conclude with a dozen time-tested principles for discovering God's purpose for your life. May He richly bless you as you continue on your path.

1. Remember That the Search for Purpose Is a Journey, Not a Destination: Amid your changing circumstances, God will continue to reveal Himself to you *if* you sincerely seek His will. As you journey through the stages of life, remember that every new day presents fresh opportunities to seek God's will; make the conscious effort to seize those opportunities.

2. Pray Early and Often: Start each day with a time of prayer and devotional readings. In those quiet moments, God will lead you; your task, of course, is to be still, to seek His will, and to follow His direction.

3. Quiet Please: Sometimes, God speaks to you in a quiet voice; usually, the small quiet voice inside can help you find the right path for your life; listen to that voice.

4. Use All the Tools That God Provides: As you continue to make important decisions about your future, read God's Word every day, and consult with trusted advisors whom God has seen fit to place along your path.

5. Take Sensible Risks in Pursuit of Personal or Professional Growth: It is better to attempt great things and fail than to attempt nothing and succeed. But, make sure to avoid *foolish* risks. When in doubt, reread Proverbs.

6. Expect Setbacks: Your path will have many twists and turns. When you face a setback, don't become discouraged. When you encounter a roadblock, be prepared to make a U-turn. Then, start searching for a better route to your chosen destination.

7. Use Your Experiences As Valued Instructors: Philosopher George Santayana correctly observed, "Those who cannot remember the past are condemned to repeat it." Act accordingly.

8. Write It Down: If you're facing a big decision, or if you're searching for greater fulfillment from your everyday life, begin keeping a daily journal. During quiet moments, make a written record of your thoughts, your goals, your hopes, and your concerns. The simple act of writing down your thoughts will help you clarify your ideas and your plans.

9. Don't Settle for Second, Third, or Fourth Best: God has big plans for you. Don't let Him down.

10. Serve Where You Stand: Even if you're not where you want to be, you can serve God exactly where you are. So don't underestimate the importance of your present work, and don't wait for a better day to serve God.

11. Find Pursuits About Which You Are Passionate: Find work that you love and causes that you believe in. You'll do your best when you become so wrapped up in something that you forget to call it work.

12. Have Faith and Get Busy:
Remember the words of Cyrus Curtis:
"Believe in the Lord and he will do half the
work—the last half."

_____

Every experience God gives us,
every person he puts in our lives,
is the perfect preparation for the future
that only he can see.

Corrie ten Boom